COMING OUT
AS
MENTALLY ILL

JASON BLAKE

ISBN: 978-0-9977116-4-6 (ebook)

Front cover image by Elena Dimitrova.
Book design by Damonza.com.

Printed by Laki Press in the United States of America.

First printing edition 2019.

Laki Press
2110 Kaneka St. 160
Lihue, HI 96766

www.jasonblakebooks.com

A note on language in this book

Language evolves over time, and we become more careful with it. Currently, professionals refer to people with some form of mental illness as "a person with depression" or "a person living with schizophrenia," or whatever the diagnosis is. This is currently the highest and best way to describe someone who has a mental illness.

Several times in this book, however, I state something like, "I am mentally ill." I recognize this is not the current best practice of the professional psychological community and that it would be unkind to refer to another in that way. I specifically use this slightly irreverent phrasing in this book for the purpose of removing the stigma and shame associated with mental illness. For decades, LGBTQ+ people have been called gay, queer, faggot, dyke, and so on. The people in those communities have started to self-identify with those words as a way to take back the power that had been used in those verbal assaults. That is why so often in this book I state, "I am mentally ill." Mental illness should not be stigmatized or shamed. It should be learned about, treated, and ultimately managed as a form of empowerment for the individuals and their loved ones living with it.

INTRODUCTION

My name is Jason Blake. I am mentally ill.

I'm in a unique position to come out as mentally ill. I'm an adult living in my own household, so I can't be kicked out or told to just pray it away. I'm self-employed, so I cannot be fired for admitting I'm mentally ill. I have my own business health insurance, so my coverage cannot be denied or canceled as I seek treatment for mental illness. I live in a state that is not perfect, but has some public resources for mental illness that other states do not.

As I begin to write this, I am forty-seven years old. I have lived as an openly gay man since I was about twenty-four years old. Coming out as gay or queer is often a process of a couple of years. One starts by telling one's closest friends, then moves onto a larger circle of friends and family. I believe I had "outed" myself as gay, in one way or another, by age twenty-four.

Coming out is just the beginning. Coming out is letting go of the corrosive secret that can ruin a psyche and a life if it is never handled properly. Self-acceptance can take longer based on the individual. Eventually there can be what is called gay or queer "pride." Gay pride is often misunderstood as some type of boastfulness. It's not. Gay pride is saying, "I'm really okay with who I am, and there happen to be some pretty awesome things about being me and being queer."

I was diagnosed with depression, anxiety, and ADHD approximately a decade ago. Despite what some extremists may try to peddle, these illnesses have nothing to do with the fact that I'm gay. But I brought up my sexual identity for a reason. The purpose of this book is to encourage the same wave of coming out with mental illness that has happened with sexual and gender identity in the Western world over the past fifty or so years.

At first I had no idea that I suffered from any mental illness. I only realized that despite my best efforts, my life did not work. I was not professionally successful, and this led, I believed, to great unhappiness and undue stress in my closest relationships. It also separated me from consistently showing up in society in vibrant ways.

Eventually I decided it was time for professional help. I visited my primary care physician and asked for a referral to a local psychiatrist. After several sessions of weekly talk therapy, I asked the psychiatrist if he believed I would be helped by medication. He responded that if I was open to it, it might be worth a try.

I'll explain more of my personal story later in the book. For now, I just want you to know that within a year of being treated for mental illness, my career and relationship were more stable than they had ever been. A decade later, I'm successful by conventional standards: I've been in a stable, committed relationship for eighteen years. I have an enviable income in a self-employed business and have written several books. My husband, Philip, and I own our own home and vacation a couple of times each year. I'm living the American Dream at a time when many Americans feel it is out of reach. I recognize how fortunate I am and do not take it for granted. Some of my success was caused by luck, timing, and a bit of serendipity. But I attribute at least half of my success to owning, learning about, and managing my mental illness.

My goal with this book is to improve the state of the world by starting with you.

- Do you know what mental health is?

- Are you holding on to ignorant and inaccurate beliefs about mental illness that do not serve you?

- Have you ever considered that you might be mentally ill, or have been mentally ill in the past?

- If you are or have been mentally ill, are you caring for yourself with best practices?

- Can you "come out" as mentally ill to help yourself, and ultimately society at large?

- Is there someone in your life who is mentally ill that you could help to get treatment or to "come out"?

- Do you vote in a way that empowers society to successfully treat physical and mental illness?

In some places and circumstances in the United States, it still is not safe or smart to come out publicly or privately as LGBTQ+. But it's still wise to get in touch with who you are, take care of yourself, and make plans to eventually come out fully in order for your life to work. If you suspect you have had episodes of mental illness, you may not be able to fully come out as mentally ill. But you can get educated. You can learn to take better care of yourself and your loved ones affected by your illness. And you can strategize how to put yourself in a better position that benefits you personally, your loved ones, and society at large. I hope by reading this book you will in some small way join me in taking up this flag at this critical time in history.

Coming out as mentally ill, at least to oneself, is extremely empowering. I cannot be shamed about my mental illness. I can manage my life in a way that allows me to continue to succeed and expand. I can be kind to others in a way I never imagined, because I understand the suffering and complexity of mental illness. I can plan my life in a way that takes care of my illness and allows me to grow at the same time. This is my wish for you and your loved ones. Denial, ignorance, and resistance to mental illness all have negative consequences. Coming out as mentally ill allows one to live fully and contribute to society. This leads to success and happiness. Read on to learn more.

1

WHAT IS MENTAL ILLNESS?

MENTAL ILLNESS MANIFESTS in different ways, and it takes a trained practitioner to help a person identify and manage mental illness.

For me, the biggest symptom was that life was hard. It was capital-H hard every day that I remember. Looking back over my lifetime, I started as a sullen child. Then I was an extremely willful and moody teenager, and my moodiness extended into adulthood.

Along the way, I tried to reduce the suffering of everyday life. I exercised excessively, abused alcohol, embraced my Catholicism, and prayed the Rosary. I diligently worked through at least half a dozen self-help book programs. I tried Transcendental Meditation, yoga, more advanced ayurvedic practices, *A Course In Miracles*, and a worldwide "self-development course." Before I sought professional help, I would wake up around five or five thirty in the morning, meditate for at least a half hour, write at least three pages in a journal, use affirmations, and start the day with an early morning seaside walk. My friend Peggy and I coined a phrase for that period: I was a "self-help-aholic." It took a gargantuan amount of effort to get my mood out of the basement every day, and constant vigilance to keep it from sliding back down.

Yet I never understood what all this truly meant. I was not really educated about mental illness, nor had anyone ever expressed to me that I might be struggling with depression. To me, mental illness was something "crazy" people experienced. It wasn't what I was going through. I didn't understand enough about mental illness to recognize it in myself.

The American Psychiatric Association defines mental illness as "health conditions involving changes in emotion, thinking or behavior (or a combination of these). Mental illnesses are associated with distress and/or problems functioning in social, work or family activities."[1]

Such a broad definition is required because the span of identified mental disorders is great. From a practical point of view, though, and for the average person, I believe it's simpler to define mental illness as a lack of mental health.

Of course, this brings up the question, "What *is* mental health?" The World Health Organization defines mental health as "a state of well-being in which every individual realizes his or her potential, can cope with the normal stresses of life, can work productively and fruitfully, and is able to make a contribution to his or her community."[2] I was working really hard at all these efforts, but the truth is, I wasn't making significant progress.

I think rather than immediately taking on the burden of asking "Am I mentally ill?" it's much easier to start with "Am I experiencing any lack of mental health?" or "Would I enjoy greater mental health?" While many people eschew the label "mentally ill," reaching for greater mental health might be a gentler step into the pool.

My official diagnosis is chronic depression and anxiety clustered with ADHD (attention deficit hyperactivity disorder). I remember a conversation I had with my psychiatrist after I had been in therapy and taking medication for several months. I kept referring to diagnoses like narcissism and schizophrenia as "mental illness" with a negative tone of voice. Gently, my psychiatrist said, "You know, depression is also mental illness." It landed like a rock in my gut at the time: *I am mentally ill.* It was temporarily devastating. It was also the beginning of recognizing that I had been protecting my ego even while being treated. Other people were mentally ill, not me.

Treatment and education eventually led to a sounder belief system: Yes, I am mentally ill. I'm a person who has mental illness but successfully manages it. This allows me to thrive in my profession, my relationship, and my community. I'm proud to be managing my mental illness and not having my mental illness manage me.

Could you be suffering from mental illness? The National Alliance on Mental Illness (NAMI) identifies the following warning signs:[3]

- Excessive worrying or fear
- Feeling excessively sad or low
- Confused thinking or problems concentrating and learning
- Extreme mood changes, including uncontrollable "highs" or feelings of euphoria
- Prolonged or strong feelings of irritability or anger
- Avoiding friends and social activities
- Difficulties understanding or relating to other people
- Changes in sleeping habits or feeling tired and low energy
- Changes in eating habits such as increased hunger or lack of appetite
- Changes in sex drive
- Difficulty perceiving reality (delusions or hallucinations, in which a person experiences and senses things that don't exist in objective reality)
- Inability to perceive changes in one's own feelings, behavior or personality ("lack of insight" or anosognosia)
- Abuse of substances like alcohol or drugs
- Multiple physical ailments without obvious causes (such as headaches, stomach aches, vague and ongoing "aches and pains")
- Thinking about suicide

- Inability to carry out daily activities or handle daily problems and stress

- An intense fear of weight gain or concern with appearance

The idea I had of depression and the typical warning signs of depression that you hear about—suicidal thoughts, decreased energy, weight changes, major mood changes— none of these were apparent to me. The feelings I'd had for most of my life did not seem depressed to me. They seemed like the way life was. I didn't think about suicide, had no trouble getting out of bed, and worked hard every day.

What was real for me, though, and what drove me to treatment, was a type of futility in what I perceived to me just hard luck results. No matter how diligently I worked in life, I was not achieving anywhere near the professional goals I had hoped to reach. I wanted a more rewarding career, and I wanted to make more money. There was a large gap between what I imagined as my potential and what my actual life looked like. This gap took a huge psychological toll on my self-esteem. Only after months of unraveling did I start to realize that the emotional volatility I experienced day in and day out, primarily internally, might not be just the way life was. There might be a level of stability and gentle joy that could be a normal place from which to start each day. This was something I couldn't even imagine as I began treatment.

If you have children who are still learning to define and talk about their emotions, NAMI points out that mental illness in children often begin with behavioral changes like these:

- Changes in school performance
- Excessive worry or anxiety (for instance, fighting to avoid bed or school)
- Hyperactive behavior
- Frequent nightmares
- Frequent disobedience or aggression
- Frequent temper tantrums[4]

I read an article recently that said anxiety in children often shows up as stomach upset. It reminded me that for at least a decade in my childhood, I was told by loved ones that I had "a nervous stomach." I frequently had stomach aches and diarrhea. I don't think anyone in my family ever knew those were early signs of my depression and anxiety. We treated the symptoms, not the cause.

Are you as mentally healthy as you'd like to be? If in any respect the answer is "no" or "maybe not," for you or any of your loved ones, keep reading.

2

THE NUMBERS

BEFORE I KNEW that I was mentally ill, in my worldview mental illness was never common or understated. My ideas of mental illness were drawn from movies like *One Flew Over the Cuckoo's Nest, Sybil,* and *Psycho.* Mental illness was also very black and white in my mind, never gray or subtle. "Mentally ill" was what I thought about homeless people on park benches, people whose drug abuse left them estranged from their families, people in long-term psychiatric wards at hospitals, and pedophiles. Mental illness was not something that afflicted "normal" or "everyday" people. When I was growing up, terms like postpartum depression and PTSD were not commonplace where I lived as they are societally now. I was part of the Oprah generation that was just starting to get secrets out into the light of day. In my view, mental illness was not widespread or inconspicuous. Rather, it was rare and always extreme.

During my process of getting educated, I learned that nothing could be further from the truth. Mental illness is at an epidemic level in America and the rest of the Western world. Here are some statistics from the National Alliance on Mental Illness:

- Approximately one in five adults in America experiences mental illness in a given year.

- Of all the Americans who experience a substance use disorder, more than one third also have a mental illness.

- At least 46 percent of homeless people live with mental illness and/or substance use disorders.

- At least 20 percent of incarcerated individuals have a recent history of a mental health condition.[5]

Suicide is also at record levels in America. Suicide is currently the tenth leading cause of death, and nearly 47,000 people committed suicide in 2017 alone. The suicide rate has increased steadily over the past decade.[6] In recent years, the epidemic of suicide has been highlighted by celebrity suicides including Kate Spade, Anthony Bourdain, and Margot Kidder. Indeed, "having it all" doesn't necessarily mean that everything is okay.

Many mental health professionals also believe that the President of the United States elected in 2016 exhibits the behavior of severe and worsening mental illness.[7]

The societal costs of mental illness are huge. Serious mental illness costs America over $193 billion in lost earnings every year. People with serious mental illness are much more likely to have other chronic health conditions. Suicide is the third leading cause of death for children aged ten to fourteen and the second leading cause of death for people aged fifteen to twenty-four. More than 90 percent of people who die by suicide have a mental health condition. And every day, an estimated eighteen to twenty-two veterans die by suicide in the United States.[8]

Globally, the numbers are even more staggering. According to *The World Health Report 2001—Mental Health: New Understanding, New Hope* from the World Health Organization (WHO):

- At least one in four people in the world will be affected by mental or neurological disorders at some point in their lives.

- At the time of the report, around 450 million people suffered from such conditions, placing mental disorders among the leading causes of ill health and disability worldwide.

- Nearly two-thirds of people with a known mental disorder never seek help from a health professional.

- Stigma, discrimination, and neglect are the leading barriers to treatment.[9]

The World Health Organization has sought to encourage governments around the world to make treating mental illness a priority. On the release of the 2001 report, Dr. Gro Harlem Brundtland, who was then Director-General of WHO, stated, "Mental illness is not a personal failure. In fact, if there is a failure, it is to be found in the way we have responded to people with mental and brain disorders."

The goal of this report was to create more action in governments. It pointed out that, at the time, 40 percent of countries had no mental health policy, over 30 percent had no mental health program, and around 25 percent had no mental health legislation.[10]

My goal with this book is to start change with individuals and families. As we become more aware and educated, we'll advocate more for ourselves and others. Advocacy leads to policy change. Policy change leads to more care, resources, and understanding.

Do you think you could become more mentally healthy? How will you get there? Are you aware of others in your life who could become more mentally healthy? How can you help them? The people in your life need you, and the world needs you.

3

TYPES OF MENTAL ILLNESSES

PRIOR TO COMING out as mentally ill, I had the poorest understanding of the most common types of mental illnesses. I had a basic concept of diseases like paranoid schizophrenia and Tourette's Syndrome, but these were derived mainly from media sources and were not comprehensive understandings. I was incredibly ignorant about the mental illnesses that affect most people—depression, anxiety disorders, ADHD, autism, and bipolar disorder. I had to learn that depression might include sadness, but might not. I had to learn that some people with ADHD are unable to focus, but others experience hyperfocus and inability to shift attention, like they are being driven by a machine. I had to learn that often mental illnesses cluster, that it's not uncommon to have more than one diagnosis. I had to learn that mental acuity and mental illness are not mutually exclusive.

The first part of coming out as mentally ill was getting

educated by experts and sound, credible resources instead of relying on the media or other uninformed individuals' opinions. Learning about mental illness is an ongoing process. I also had to come to terms with the fact that most people are not adequately informed about mental illness, so I might have to ignore the opinions of people I loved, especially if their ideas were based more on opinion than knowledge.

Unlike diabetes or cancer, mental illness currently has no specific medical tests that lead to a definitive diagnosis. For those seeking treatment for mental health, the first step is usually a thorough physical exam, including a blood panel. If other medical causes of symptoms are ruled out. the person is generally referred to a therapist, psychologist, or psychiatrist to seek diagnosis and treatment of any mental disease.

Most professional mental health workers in America use two classification systems for mental illnesses. The *Diagnostic and Statistical Manual of Mental Disorders*, fifth edition (*DSM-5*) is published by the American Psychiatric Association. The *International Classification of Diseases*, tenth edition (*ICD-10*) is published by the World Health Organization. Both are evolving classification systems, and both have been criticized at times.

These two classification systems use technical language because they're written for medical professionals. Simpler descriptions are more helpful for the rest of us, as long as they come from reliable sources.

Common Mental Disorders

The following descriptions of common mental disorders have been adapted from the website of the National Alliance of Mental Illness, with their permission.

Attention deficit hyperactivity disorder (ADHD) involves significant problems with attention, hyperactivity, or acting impulsively.

Anxiety disorders may be present when anxiety becomes overwhelming and repeatedly impacts one's life.

Autism spectrum disorder (ASD) makes it difficult to socialize or communicate with others.

Bipolar disorder causes dramatic highs and lows in a person's mood, energy, and ability to think clearly.

Depression is more than feeling sad or going through a rough patch; it's a serious mental health condition that requires understanding and treatment.

Psychosis is characterized as disruptions to thoughts and perceptions that makes it difficult for the person to recognize what is real and what isn't.

Eating disorders occur when extreme preoccupation with food and weight issues make it difficult for the person to focus on other aspects of life.

Obsessive-compulsive disorder (OCD) causes repetitive, unwanted, intrusive thoughts and irrational, excessive urges to do certain actions.

Posttraumatic stress disorder (PTSD) is the result of traumatic events such as military combat, assault, an accident, or a natural disaster.

Schizophrenia causes people to lose touch with reality, often in the forms of hallucinations, delusions, and extremely disordered thinking and behavior.[11]

Personality Disorders

An additional classification of mental illnesses is known as personality disorders. The American Psychiatric Association describes them as "a way of thinking, feeling and behaving that deviates from the expectations of the culture, causes distress or problems functioning and lasts over time." Some of the personality disorders described on the APA website include the following (reproduced with their permission):

Antisocial personality disorder is a pattern of disregarding or violating the rights of others. A person with antisocial personality disorder may not conform to social norms, may repeatedly lie or deceive others, or may act impulsively.

Borderline personality disorder is a pattern of instability in personal relationships, intense emotions, poor self-image, and impulsivity. A person with borderline personality disorder may go to great lengths to avoid being abandoned, have repeated suicide attempts, display inappropriate intense anger, or have ongoing feelings of emptiness.

Narcissistic personality disorder is a pattern of need for admiration and lack of empathy for others. A person with narcissistic personality disorder may have a grandiose sense of self-importance, a sense of entitlement, take advantage of others, or lack empathy.

Paranoid personality disorder is a pattern of being suspicious of others and seeing them as mean or spiteful. People with paranoid personality disorder often assume people will harm or deceive them and don't confide in others or become close to them.[12]

Substance Use Disorders

The National Institute of Mental Health (NIMH) considers substance use disorders (often called substance abuse) as a mental illness. As stated on NIMH's website, "Substance use disorder changes normal desires and priorities. It changes normal behaviors and interferes with the ability to work, go to school, and to have good relationships with friends and family."[13] In 2014, about 39 percent of US adults who had a substance use disorder also had another mental illness.[14]

Conclusion

This is by no means an exhaustive list of the types of mental disorders. Also keep in mind that most mental illnesses occur on a spectrum from mild to severe, and they can be episodic (happening once or just occasionally) or chronic (long-term).

The purpose of these and other diagnoses isn't to stigmatize or pigeonhole yourself or another individual. Rather, a diagnosis is a pointer toward treatments that have been successful for other individuals over time, helping them manage their symptoms to experience greater mental health. Our ability to precisely diagnose and treat mental illness becomes stronger and better as the body of evidence grows and new and better treatments are discovered.

4

THE CAUSES OF
MENTAL ILLNESS

MY FIRST RESPONSE to being identified as mentally ill was a great feeling of shame. Some of the unhelpful beliefs I shared in my journal included:

- If you're taking medication, you're just lazy and unwilling to do the real (emotional or self-help) work.

- Mental illness is ultimately the result of a lack of personal integrity on my part.

- I should be able to handle all mental problems through self-help, diet, and exercise.

- Medication would leave me numb and zombie-like.

- By taking medication, I'd be supporting Big Pharma, which is corrupt and only wants people to get hooked on medicines without any real care for the long-term effects.

- Something is wrong with me if I am mentally ill, and that means I am personally to blame.

These are just some of the destructive, inaccurate thoughts I had at the time. There are bits of truth in some them, but all of them lack any nuance. As I studied more, I discovered more about mental illness that was true, based on facts and science, and sometimes complex. Each new discovery removed the feeling of shame and gave me powerful knowledge to move forward with.

We have less research and less data on the causes of mental illness compared to other chronic diseases, such as diabetes or heart disease. But research continues, and we are learning more every day.

Most mental illnesses have a combination of biological, psychological, and environmental causes. According to an article on WebMD:

> Some mental illnesses have been linked to abnormal functioning of nerve cell circuits or pathways that connect particular brain regions. Nerve cells within these brain circuits communicate through chemicals called neurotransmitters. "Tweaking" these chemicals—through medicines, psychotherapy or other medical procedures—can help brain circuits run more efficiently. In addition, defects in or injury to certain areas of the brain have also been linked to some mental conditions.[15]

The article explains that genetics play a role. A person can inherit a predisposition to a certain mental illness. That susceptibility, when combined with the right trigger—a stress, abuse, or traumatic event—can influence the development of a mental illness. Other biological causes of mental illness include infections, brain injuries or defects, substance abuse, and even poor nutrition.

Psychological causes of mental illness can include childhood psychological trauma, such as emotional, physical, or sexual abuse. They can also include early losses, like the loss of a parent, neglect, and poor social conditioning.

Environmentally, certain stressors can trigger mental illness in those who are susceptible to it. Those stressors might be events like death or divorce; dysfunctional family life; negative feelings like low self-esteem, anxiety, anger, or loneliness; changing jobs or schools; social or cultural expectations; and substance abuse by the person or those close to him or her.[16]

In his book *What Is Mental Illness?*, psychology professor Richard McNally points out that the biological causes of some mental disorders, such as schizophrenia, bipolar disorder, and autism, can be seen using methods such as imaging scans. "Yet for other conditions, such as depression or anxiety, the biological foundation is more nebulous," he writes. "Often, mental illnesses are likely to have multiple causes, including genetic, biological and environmental factors. Of course, that's true for many chronic diseases, heart disease and diabetes included. But for mental illnesses, we're a particularly long way from understanding the interplay among those factors."[17]

There are positive trends that indicate we'll become better at diagnosing mental illnesses. For example:

- More governments are funding psychiatric research as they recognize the costs of not addressing mental illness.

- Pharmaceutical companies recognize there are still unmet needs and are seeking better and more specific treatments for mental conditions.

- New technologies like gene editing, synthetic biology, and nanotechnology offer promise to medicine at large, including the diagnosis and treatment of mental illnesses.

- New technologies like biosensors, artificial intelligence, and machine learning will enable earlier detection and diagnosis of mental illness.[18]

As with all diseases, as stigma falls away, society invests more in scientific study for diagnosis and treatment. As new and better approaches prevail, we'll be able to make access to mental health care more available and affordable. There is hope.

5

GETTING EDUCATED AND GETTING HELP

IN MY JOURNEY of coming out as mentally ill, just like coming out as gay, I had to recruit advocates at first, as well as be careful with whom I shared this information. For instance, my spouse and a couple of very close friends were the only people I told that I was starting an antidepressant. I already knew a couple of family members had negative views of antidepressants, and I was busy correcting my own beliefs. I also was in a competitive work environment where the information could have been used against me negatively. It's important as one comes out to recruit good supporters. As I became more stable, I was comfortable sharing the information with more and more people. In fact, over time a few people told me that my coming out as mentally ill encouraged them to handle some of their own mental health issues.

Access to help can vary drastically depending on where you live. For instance, when I started working with a psychiatrist, there were only two on my tiny island, and only one of them was accepting new patients. There's a wealth of books that provide information about mental illness, but our island didn't have a big bookstore, and the library only had outdated copies of the books I wanted to read. Often I had to order them online or download them in an electronic format.

You may have limited access to health insurance, health care providers, or both. But there are ways to get help even with limited resources. Sometimes a good therapist is knowledgeable about medications and can work in tandem with a family doctor. Many communities have government-funded mental health centers where fees are waived or charged on a sliding scale. There's even therapy available online that may cost less than the copay for an in-office therapy appointment.

The main lesson with mental health is the same as for physical health: you must be your own advocate. This means doing research. It means talking to professionals about what is available. It means if you hit a wall, you don't just give up—you turn in another direction and look for another solution.

Here's an interesting story about access to care: I've been seeing my primary care physician for about fourteen years. He's the one who got me my first psychiatrist appointment.

Recently we talked about mental health. He was frustrated that he had no one to refer his patients to when they needed mental health care. I told him that a couple of years ago, I discovered that our state has a mental health access line. If someone calls and goes through a phone screening, he or she can immediately get one month of psychiatric care for free. If the mental illness diagnosis is considered severe, the care is ongoing, regardless of income or insurance. Until we discussed it, my doctor had no idea this service existed. He wrote down the number and was relieved he had another resource for patients. If I had stopped looking for help, I never would have found this service, and I certainly would not have been able to share it with my physician.

Here are the basics of getting help. First of all, if you are in crisis or having suicidal thoughts, you can get help by calling the National Suicide Prevention Lifeline at 1-800-273-8255 or by going to the closest emergency room.

Beyond that, there are many ways to get started on a journey toward greater mental health, depending on how you want to begin. I recognize that our healthcare system in America is fragmented and disparate, and that mental health care is often much less readily available than care for other illnesses. With that said, there are always some positive steps you can take.

The National Alliance on Mental Illness website (*www. nami.org*) has good information about where and how to get help. Importantly, NAMI points out that there is no "one size fits all" treatment plan for any mental illness. Choosing the right treatment plan for you is important, and your plan may need to evolve over time. Those who can help with assessment and therapy include doctorate-level psychologists and masters-level counselors, clinicians, therapists, and clinical social workers. Those who can prescribe and monitor medications include psychiatrists, psychiatric nurse practitioners, primary care physicians, and family nurse practitioners. Other professionals who can still provide help or point patients in the right direction include certified peer specialists, social workers, and pastoral counselors.

For ongoing mental health treatment, different settings exist, although they may or may not be available in your area. The most common are professional private practices of therapists or psychiatrists, community or county mental health centers, and substance abuse treatment centers.

The best practice for treating many mental health conditions is a combination of psychotherapy and medication. Psychotherapy, or "talk therapy," can be effective at improving symptoms for many types of mental illness. It involves speaking with a trained therapist in a safe and confidential environment to explore and understand feelings and behaviors and gain coping skills. Talk therapy can be used for individuals, couples, families, and groups.

Psychiatric medicines influence the brain chemicals that regulate emotions and thought patterns. They are most effective when combined with talk therapy. Predicting what medication will work best for a patient is more of an art than an exact science. Persistence is encouraged until one finds the best medications and dosages to help. Changes take weeks to be noticed. It's important to stay in good communication with the prescriber while working toward the right treatment. Also, it's just as important to receive help when going off a medication, since side effects can be severe. In some cases, medication may be short-term. In others, it can be required for a lifetime.

Complementary health approaches include services that are not FDA reviewed or approved. These treatments can range from dietary choices and supplement additions to mind-body treatments like yoga, meditation, or tai chi. Any complementary treatments should be discussed in detail with one's regular mental health doctor, since they can sometimes interfere with traditional forms of treatment.19

When treatments such as medication and talk therapy are not relieving symptoms, brain stimulating therapies like electroconvulsive therapy (ECT) or transcranial magnetic stimulation (TMS) may provide relief.20

The hunt for new and more effective treatments continues nonstop. There is even compelling data that certain psychedelic compounds, such as psilocybin, may help in cases where more traditional treatment has not.21 Have a detailed discussion with your health care providers about the range of treatments and possibilities that may be most effective for you.

6

UNDERSTANDING AND DISMANTLING THE STIGMA

PRIOR TO GETTING educated and getting treatment, I personally added to the stigma of mental illness. Here are some of the ways I did this:

- In high school, a friend and I joked about her mom's therapy and treatment with lithium.

- For decades, I believed depression was primarily a spiritual issue. When I was a practicing Catholic, I believed mental illness to be the result of sin or a lack of prayer. Later in life, when I was part of a "self-development course," I believed depression was solely the result of unhelpful beliefs and integrity issues.

- I considered all substance abuse issues mainly a result of lack of willpower.

- As is common in society, I referred to people as "crazy" or "nuts" or "cuckoo." I often mocked people who probably were suffering, rather than choosing to educate myself and feel compassion.

- I assumed that mental illness was something that could be more easily handled with exercise, diet, and good habits than with medication.

I'm sure there are other examples. The primary problem was that I assumed I knew things about which I was actually woefully ignorant. My full-throated opinions had almost nothing to do with science or the body of knowledge accumulated over decades by professionals. A lack of education was my biggest mistake. Have you participated in increasing the stigma around mental illness?

In the United States, there is still great stigma with identifying oneself as mentally ill. Societal attitudes about mental illness are overgeneralized or false. When those suffering with mental illness self-stigmatize by internalizing those negative attitudes and beliefs, they suffer as a result.

According to a 2016 study on the origins of societal stigma toward mental illness:

- Throughout history, those suffering from mental illness were often treated the same way as slaves or criminals.

- Mental illness has often been equated with punishment from God or a sign of possession.

- During the Middle Ages, those with mental illness were often burned at the stake or imprisoned in a madhouse, where they were often chained to the walls or beds.

- Nazi Germany murdered and sterilized hundreds of thousands of mentally ill people.

- The most prominent stigmas about the mentally ill are that they are dangerous, unpredictable, or unreliable.

- Even as children, we are taught to quickly label people as "crazy," "weird," or "nuts."

- Media coverage of mental illness has been consistently and overwhelmingly negative and imprecise.

- Healthcare professionals sometimes have even stronger and more negative views of people with mental illness than the general population does.

- Stigma leads to avoidance of treatment or a lack of compliance with prescribed medication.

- Self-stigma can lead to lower self-esteem and self-efficacy.

- "Courtesy stigma" occurs when the stigma surrounding a mentally ill individual transfers to the professional and familial relationships surrounding the person. Just as affected people experience self-stigma, these people can also experience shame and guilt, blaming themselves for somehow contributing to the illness.[22]

Some research suggests that the stigma of mental illness is making us sicker:

- Worldwide, 60 percent of people with mental

illness receive no care. In developing countries, that figure jumps to 90 percent.

- The stigma of mental illness leads to what is called social distancing, resulting in isolation and loneliness, both of which can exacerbate mental illness.

- People with mental illness are ten times more likely to be in prison than in psychiatric facilities.[23]

So where does this leave us? Luna Greenstein, in an article on the NAMI website, shares these practices to fight mental health stigma:

- Talk openly about mental health.

- Educate yourself and others.

- Be conscious of your language and others' language around mental illness. Make corrections where needed.

- Encourage equality between physical illness and mental illness.

- Show compassion for those with mental illness.

- Choose empowerment over shame.

- Be honest about treatment.

- Let the media know when they're being stigmatizing.

- Don't harbor self-stigma.[24]

Most people can work to reduce their own contribution to the stigmatization of mental illness and to dismantle the societal stigma. Mind yourself, and speak up when someone else can do better.

7

BRIDGING THE DIVIDE

As I became educated and underwent treatment, I originally was tight-lipped about my mental illness and depression. Eventually, when I was seeing results in both how I felt and the success of my life, I knew that to correct my previous ignorance, I needed to be a voice.

I began in small ways. When someone said something negative about antidepressants, I spoke up and stated that my life had been greatly improved by them. When people I cared about shared a wealth of problems that seemed more than just circumstantial, I asked them if they'd considered talking to a therapist or at least discussing their symptoms with their doctor. I noticed that the more I opened up about my mental health challenges, the more people around me would also open up. They shared stories of their depression or family members who struggled with mental illness. They shared that it didn't feel okay to talk about mental illness. This book was the natural next step in helping to end the stigma and bridge the divide.

We all know someone who would rush to their doctor or an urgent care clinic at the first sniffle of an allergy or a cold, but who would never consider getting a mental health evaluation or scheduling an appointment to speak to a therapist. Why is that? It's partly due to the stigma about mental health. But I'd also argue that Western culture leans toward a focus on pragmatic, action-based behavior rather than introspection and "going within." These cultural norms then lead to policies that make mental health care less available and effective than our already imperfect system for healing the physical body.

Consider this, though: How likely is it that someone suffering from major depression will be able to stay on their medication to treat other conditions, such as heart disease and diabetes? Probably not very likely.

According to the key findings of a British report published in 2016:

> Efforts to develop integrated care should focus more on the integration of physical and mental health, addressing in particular four major challenges:
>
> - High rates of mental health conditions among people with long-term physical health problems.
>
> - Poor management of "medically unexplained symptoms," which lack an identifiable organic cause.

- Reduced life expectancy among people with the most severe forms of mental illness, largely attributable to poor physical health.

- Limited support for the wider psychological aspects of physical health and illness.[25]

The divide in how physical and mental illness are treated even comes from within the healthcare community. In our local newspaper, a retired family physician wrote an op-ed discouraging people from ever using medication for mental health issues. He said exercise and psychotherapy were the only real answers. The main reasons he gave for avoiding medication for mental health were:

- The drugs have side effects, sometimes severe.

- Sometimes they don't work, and one must increase dosage or change to a new medication.

- The treatment plans can be complicated.

- One may have to stay on these medications for life.

I was flabbergasted by these statements. Though I am not a doctor, I work in health care with the senior population. What was striking to me is that the writer's stated reasons for not seeking prescription drug treatment would also apply to other common diseases like heart disease, hypertension, diabetes, and hyperthyroidism. For all these diseases and others, it's true that medications can have side effects. The patient then works with the physician to find the right medicine and dosage for maximum effectiveness and reduced side effects. When needed, physicians change medicines and dosages to better treat these physical illnesses.

And generally, without major lifestyle changes around diet and exercise—some of which still may not be effective—most people take these medications for life.

I further discussed this op-ed with my psychiatrist. He shared several practical reasons to use medication to treat mental illness. For example, someone with major depression who can't get out of bed, manage hygiene, or make normal appointments probably isn't yet able to commit to normal exercise and talk therapy sessions. Sometimes the patient's symptoms, level of commitment, or other personal characteristics can prevent talk therapy from being successful. And many mental illnesses may not respond well to talk therapy alone, so medication is the best way to stabilize the patient to increase the chance of succeeding in therapy.

The 2016 British report cited earlier outlines ten areas that are ripe for improvement to integrate mental and physical health care:

- Incorporating mental health into public health programs.

- Promoting health among people with severe mental illnesses.

- Improving management of medically unexplained symptoms in primary care.

- Strengthening primary care for the physical health needs of people with severe mental illnesses.

- Supporting the mental health of people with long-term physical health conditions.

- Supporting the mental health and well-being of caregivers.

- Supporting mental health in hospitals.

- Addressing physical health in mental health inpatient facilities.

- Providing integrated support for perinatal mental health.

- Supporting the mental health needs of people in residential homes.[26]

The other remarkable thing about this report is that it comes from a relatively small country that has universal health care. The problems are even more severe and urgent when you consider the health care system in the United States. Under the current system, not all people have health coverage; availability of treatment varies widely due to location and socioeconomic position; the system is fragmented, with not all providers working with all insurance companies; price controls on prescription drugs are nonexistent; and a profit motive exists in many layers of the system, potentially benefitting service providers more than patients.

Moving in the direction of this more integrated healthcare system, giving equal weight to mental and physical conditions, is a heavy lift. But it is also the only sane direction for our society. The steps to bridging this divide are clear but not easy:

- Promoting self-awareness and care of one's own physical and mental health.

- Becoming more aware of the divide between

mental and physical health and encouraging those around us to take a more integrated approach to health care.

- Working daily to reduce stigma around mental health care and its inclusion as part of physical care.

- Advocating—locally, at the state level, and nationally—public policy that results in more integrated and available care and greater public willingness to embrace treatment.

As I read through what I've just written, it sounds like a huge societal burden. Words and phrases like inertia, special interests, apathy, an overworked and underinformed society—very depressing thoughts—pop up in my mind. But what turns the table on those thoughts is that if the radical individual and societal changes recommended by experts are implemented, in the long run we will ultimately reduce the costs of care for all of us, leading to greater well-being, longer lives, and more productivity and prosperity for more of the world. That is something worth fighting for, even if it takes decades.

8

TOWARD GREATER COMPASSION

I've become kinder since I started managing and getting educated about my own mental health. First, I feel better, so I have more bandwidth to care more about others. Second, the more I learn, the more I realize how many people are suffering, often without any treatment and limited resources. When you start to look around for signs of mental illness and suffering, it is everywhere, in varying degrees. I no longer think of mentally ill people as "those people." I am mentally ill. When you suffer with any mental or physical ailment, you realize how precious, finite, and tenuous life is. That opens my heart and helps me care more about others. I've become a better person by virtue of dealing with my own mental illness.

This small chapter is less about clinical evidence and

resources and more about meditating on how learning about mental illness has helped me. We are human beings in a big, messy world. If you're doing anything, you interact with many different people. Things usually happen in those interactions. Many of them are wonderful. Some can be mundane. Some can be unpleasant or worse.

Consider the statistic I gave in an earlier chapter: Approximately one in five adults in America experiences mental illness in a given year. That is a huge number of people you are potentially interacting with every day of your life. And next year, the "one in five" you interact with might be a different person. The takeaway: We are all going through something emotional or difficult very often.

So what are the lessons we can learn about how to develop more compassion?

The first lesson is self-care. Notice your mental health. Do what you have to do. Journal. Talk to friends. Take walks. Exercise. Try not to yell at anyone, but if you do, apologize. If you drink too much, notice it and manage it. Practice self-care and self-kindness and do your best. Life is hard enough not to be on your own side along the way.

Lesson number two: extend that same kindness to others. If someone's having a bad day and you can't make it better, keep a polite distance. If a friend or co-worker snaps at you, it's okay to ask, "Is everything all right? Can I do anything?" Practice small, random acts of kindness. Bring donuts. Send a card. Pick up the drink tab every now and then. This is a world with a lot of suffering and heartache. That won't change soon. We must do our best to care for ourselves and one another to actively create a better life experience for all.

I used to be quick to label someone an asshole, a jerk, or a bitch. Now I have space. When I don't understand someone's actions or motives, even after taking the time to try to get more data, I always have the fallback of labeling unpleasant interactions as "unmanaged mental illness." Now, that's not an official diagnosis. And that label could easily be used with callousness. That's not what I'm talking about. Rather, I'm suggesting that when you really can't get to the heart of another person's actions, words, or behaviors, after working in good faith to do so, the idea that it might be a mental event lets you see that person as human, give them a break, and remove yourself from the situation so you don't make it worse. I liken it to Christians who say, "We're all sinners"—not as a means of condemning others, but as a way of acknowledging that thousands of variables contribute to what a person may be going through at any moment of any day.

Take care of yourself. Take care of others if you can. Do your best. Give yourself a break if your best isn't enough. Our common humanity is the only thing that really unites us and has the power to move us forward together.

9

MANAGEMENT AND STABILITY

HERE ARE THE things I currently do to manage my mental illness and stay stable and successful:

- I journal daily first thing in the morning. It seems to ground me and help me work out minor issues.

- Over time, I changed my career path and found work that better suited my personality. This was a major improvement in my life.

- On the weekend, I read my recent journal entries to see if there's anything I need to address.

- I take a relatively low dose of one antidepressant per day.

- I go to therapy once a month with my psychiatrist to check on my medication and talk through anything I'd like to discuss.

- I talk to my friends a few times throughout the week.

- If I watch or read news reports about serious issues that leave me feeling anxious or depressed, I make sure I counter them with lighter content, such as reading a novel or watching a comedy.

- I always try to have one creative project, no matter how small, moving forward in addition to my regular work life.

- I try to do one kind thing for myself every week—maybe a couple hours of scuba diving, watching a show I like, buying something small that I need, taking a walk at a favorite place—anything that is deliberate and a kindness to me from me.

- I exercise at least five days a week, usually a combination of weight training and cardio.

- I pay attention to the food I eat and try to gravitate toward choices that make me feel healthier.

- My husband and I care for two awesome dogs who love us more than we could ever imagine.

It's not a terribly difficult list, and I'm dedicated to following it. Many of these habits improve not only my mental health, but my physical health and quality of life. Most of us were taught the basics of health hygiene as children, and many adults have practices or routines that bolster their happiness and success. If you haven't considered what mental health hygiene practices you need, it might not be a bad thing to think about.

Healing is a buzz word that is, in my opinion, abused in our society. Very often the word "heal" or "healing" has a societal marketing implication. It implies that someone recovers from an illness entirely, like getting over a common cold. That is not often the case with chronic diseases. It's rare for someone with Type 2 diabetes or hypertension to completely get over it and need no more treatment or medication. Often, the real goal of proper care is to help someone manage and stabilize a disease.

This is also the goal with most types of mental illness. Marketing presents us with messages that if we just eat clean, avoid pesticides, exercise, do yoga, manage stress, and maybe even shop at the right stores, we can age gracefully, free of any illness or disease. Those things may help in some cases of mental illness, but they aren't necessarily end-all solutions. Most mental health issues last a long time. Sometimes the most adult solution is to manage one's lifestyle as best one can, but also get on board with the best treatment plan, which may continue for life.

Anecdotes and individual stories about mental illness often emphasize a resistance to medication and the goal of getting off medication completely. Part of managing illnesses as an adult is coming to terms with the idea that medication may have to be taken forever. Those with chronic hypertension know they must take those pills for the rest of their lives or risk a greater chance of a stroke or heart attack. Insulin-dependent diabetics know that going off their insulin at any point could lead to a deadly diabetic coma. The same type of maturity needs to be considered with mental illness.

Mental Health America (MHA) describes itself as "the nation's leading community-based nonprofit dedicated to addressing the needs of those living with mental illness and to promoting the overall mental health of all Americans."[27] They have created a succinct fact sheet that I believe provides great advice for managing mental illness. I have reproduced its content here with MHA's permission.

Staying Well When You Have a Mental Illness

When you have a mental illness, you may not realize how important your overall health is to your recovery. Having poor overall health can get in the way and make recovery harder. Finding ways to take care of your health can aid your recovery and help you feel better overall. Here are some things you can do.

Advocate for yourself. You deserve good health care. All too often, people with mental illnesses develop other health conditions, such as heart disease and diabetes, because their health is overlooked. If your doctor is not asking about your overall health, let him know that it's important to you and essential to your recovery.

Get the care you need. Get routine check-ups and visit your doctor when you're not feeling well. It may be due to your medicine or a symptom of your mental illness. But it could also be a different health problem.

Manage stress. Everyone has stress. It is a normal part of life. You can feel stress in your body when you have too much to do or when you haven't slept well. You can also feel stress when you worry about your job, money, relationships, or a friend or family member who is ill or in crisis. Stress can make you feel run down. It can also cause your mind to race and make it hard to focus on the things you need to do. If you have a mental illness, lots of stress can make you feel worse and make it harder to function. If you are feeling stressed, there are steps you can take to feel better:

- **Slow down and take one thing at a time.** If you feel like you have too much to do, make a list and work on it one task at a time.

- **Know your limits.** Let others know, them too. If you're overwhelmed at home or work, or with friends, learn how to say "no." It may be hard at first, so practice saying "no" with the people you trust most.

- **Practice stress reduction techniques.** There are a lot of things you can do to make your life more peaceful and calm. Do something you enjoy, exercise, connect with others or meditate.

- **Know your triggers.** What causes stress in your life? If you know where stress is coming from, you will be able to manage it better.

- **Talk to someone.** You don't have to deal with stress on your own. Talking to a trusted friend, family member, support group or counselor can make you feel better. They also may help you figure out how to better manage stress in your life.

Plan your sleep schedule. Sleep can affect your mood and your body and is important to your recovery. Not getting the right amount of sleep can make day-to-day functioning and recovery harder. For tips on how to sleep better, contact the National Sleep Foundation at 202-347-3471 or visit www.sleepfoundation.org.

Watch what you eat. Sometimes, medicine can cause you to gain weight. Other times, eating unhealthy foods can cause weight gain. Foods high in calories and saturated or "bad" fats can raise your blood pressure and cholesterol. This can increase your chances of gaining weight and having other health problems, like heart disease and diabetes. Here are some short cuts you can take to healthy eating.

- If fresh vegetables are too costly, buy frozen vegetables. They can cost less and last a long time in your freezer.

- If you eat at fast food restaurants, many now offer healthy foods such as salads or grilled chicken.

Talk to your doctor to learn more about how to have a healthy diet.

Exercise. Along with a healthy diet, exercise can improve your health and well-being. Exercising regularly can increase your self-esteem and confidence; reduce your feelings of stress, anxiety and depression; improve your sleep; and help you maintain a healthy weight.

Find a type of exercise that you enjoy and talk to your doctor. You might enjoy walking, jogging or even dancing. You don't have to go to a gym or spend money to exercise. Here are some things you can start doing now to get active:

- Check out your local community center for free, fun activities.

- Take a short walk around the block with family, friends or coworkers.

- Take the stairs instead of the elevator. Make sure the stairs are well lit.

- Turn on some music and dance.

Do something you enjoy. During the week, find time—30 minutes, a couple of hours or whatever you can fit in—to do something you enjoy. Read a book or magazine, go for a walk or spend time with friends. Taking time for yourself to have fun and laugh can help you relax, ease stress and improve the way you feel.

Connect with others. Spending time with positive, loving people you care about and trust can ease stress, help your mood and improve the way you feel overall. They may be family members, close friends, members of a support group or a counselor at the local drop-in center. Many communities even have warm lines you can call to talk to someone.

Substance Abuse

If you find yourself drinking or using drugs to cope, it is time to seek help. Although using drugs and alcohol may seem to help you cope, substance abuse can make your symptoms worse, delay your treatment and complicate recovery. It can also cause abuse or addiction problems. To find help now, call 800-662-HELP or visit www.findtreatment.samhsa.gov.

Smoking

If you smoke, talk to your doctor about quitting. Smoking puts you at risk for problems like heart disease and cancer.[28]

Like physical diseases, some mental illnesses are severe. There may not be adequate treatments for those illnesses. Some data suggests that it's difficult for people suffering with severe mental illness to stay compliant with their treatment plans. I don't want to dismiss the notion that sometimes there's not a good plan that leads to a magically happy life. My goal is simply to inspire those suffering with mental illness to do what is possible to take care of themselves.

10

SILVER LININGS

ONE THING I haven't yet revealed to you is that I'm a gifted and trained singer. It's been a hobby throughout my life. Last spring, our local community theater did a production of the musical *Sweeney Todd*. I was lucky to be cast as "the demon barber of Fleet Street" and performed the role for about a month. I think if I had never plumbed the depths of my own darkness and depression and learned to embrace and understand those parts of myself, I never would have succeeded in getting the role. As with most things, coming out as mentally ill can have positive ripple effects in ways we never consider.

As people come to terms with acknowledging, treating, and stabilizing their mental illness, they may come to discover certain "perks" of their disorders. While no one wishes to be mentally ill, managing the experience often leads to compassion for others who are living with mental illness, as well as a greater understanding of life. Just as many people who've had cancer report having learned something from that experience, mental illness may bring certain gifts or "silver linings."

After reading *Driven to Distraction: Recognizing and Coping with Attention Deficit Disorder from Childhood through Adulthood*, by Edward M. Hallowell and John J. Ratey, I came away with a very valuable, simple solution for managing my life. I learned I always need clear, inspiring goals *and* I need to know exactly what the next step is in walking toward each goal. This knowledge alone has helped me accomplish more in the last decade than I probably did in the first thirty-five years of my life.

Through therapy and education, most people find real value and understanding in learning more about their mental illness. This knowledge leads to empowerment and the ability to self-advocate, often in ways they could not do before their diagnoses. The gifts most often reported with depression include patience, humility, insight, and empathy.

For ADHD, a community has formed around what's called "the gift of ADHD." Lara Honos-Webb, a clinical psychologist, wrote a book with that title in which she encourages parents of children with ADHD to view their condition as a strength. She noted in an interview, "People of all ages who have the diagnosis of ADHD can reliably be observed to share a set of gifts including creativity, exuberance, emotional expressiveness, interpersonal intuition, ecological consciousness and leadership."[29] After my diagnosis, I read another book written by Dr. Honos-Webb, *The Gift of Adult ADD*. I came away with many insights about myself, new ways to view my disorder, and coping strategies to help me succeed and enjoy life more thoroughly.

Author and speaker Tracy Shawn, in her blog post "The Upside of Downside: The Surprising Gifts of Mental Disorders," wrote that "anxiety—with all its pain and regret—did make me stronger, more empathetic, and even more creative. It also made me that much more grateful for ordinary happiness."[30]

In the same blog post, Shawn quoted a 2012 *Wall Street Journal* article by Jonah Lehrer. He noted that "there's compelling evidence that autism is not merely a list of deficits. Rather, it represents an alternative way of making sense of the world, a cognitive difference that, in many instances, comes with unexpected benefits." Shawn continued, "Lehrer cites a study in which scientists concluded that people with autism are able to process more information in a short amount of time. . . . As Lehrer so eloquently puts it, 'What seems, at first glance, like a straightforward liability turns out to be a complex mixture of blessings and burdens.'"[31]

The ancient Greeks considered manic states to be phases of divine inspiration. In fact, an abbreviated list of famous people who have been diagnosed with bipolar disorder and have accomplished amazing things is encouraging. It includes Mel Gibson, Carrie Fisher, Catherine Zeta-Jones, Vivien Leigh, Nina Simone, Ted Turner, Ernest Hemingway, Jackson Pollack, Friedrich Nietzsche, Sir Isaac Newton, Abraham Lincoln, Virginia Woolf, Florence Nightingale, Vincent van Gogh, and others. In fact, if you or a loved one receives a diagnosis of a mental illness, I encourage you to

Google "famous people with" (insert particular disorder). The information you'll find in this endeavor will provide both inspiration and relief from a sense of isolation that can sometimes occur with mental illness.

While any mental illness or disorder will naturally come with challenges and burdens, effective treatment and management—even of severe disorders—can usually allow the person to become stable and successful. Over time, the silver linings of the situation may reveal themselves. It seems that everyone who in good faith struggles with mental illness generally becomes more humble, more compassionate, and more human. It's hard for me to see how any of those outcomes can be bad.

If you'd like to share a specific silver lining of your mental illness, contact me at *www.comingoutasmentallyill.com*.

11

THE REST OF MY MENTAL ILLNESS STORY

I'VE DROPPED SOME bits and pieces throughout the book, but thought I should share my entire "coming out as mentally ill" story. Reading it may help you understand more about what it's like to experience mental illness.

My First Realization

In my mid-thirties, I went through a host of challenges. Many of them had to do with money troubles.

Philip and I were just starting to rebuild our finances after being defrauded in a commercial real estate venture that left us bankrupt. We were relatively new to living in Hawaii, where the cost of living was high. To make things even worse, the world was going through the Great

Recession. The career I'd had in finance evaporated, and jobs in general were scarce. I applied for every opening I could, but few were available, and I rarely received any responses. At times I pieced together odd jobs with tourism-related companies. I even became a time-share salesman—a terrible career fit for me, but it was all I could find.

None of these things alone were that big of a deal. But the mental pressure they created kept piling on. After about four years of doing my best to walk a straight and narrow path, I was close to snapping. Every month, paying our rent and basic bills came down to the wire. I'd burst into tears when our well-used car had an unexpected breakdown.

One morning at about five thirty, while having coffee before getting ready for work, I wrote the following lines, almost automatically, in my journal: "Every day you write over and over in your journal about how depressed you are because you don't have any money. What if you don't have any money because of your depression?"

When I looked at the words I had just written, I was gobsmacked. Until that moment, I had never considered that I might be depressed. I didn't realize that someone who is bright could suffer from mental illness. I had been identified as gifted in elementary school, remained at the top of my class through high school, and was accepted at Georgetown University. As an adult, I had periods of solid upper-middle-class living. Those accomplishments did not fit with the limited knowledge I had about mental illness. Nor did I exhibit the common indicators of depression: I never had problems getting out of bed and going to work, and I never thought about suicide. My black moods and dark humor just felt like part of my personality.

Yet something about what I had written in my journal put me on a mission of self-discovery. It was a puzzle for me to figure out.

I discussed it with Philip at dinner that night. Did he think I might be depressed? Gently, he said that yes, on occasion he had wondered whether I was clinically depressed.

As I thought more about my mental state, I remembered having several episodes of what I thought might be manic behavior. I began to wonder whether I had bipolar disorder.

Around this time, something else happened: I injured my back and had a recurring, painful muscle spasm. My primary care physician prescribed a low dose of Valium. This prescription drug can be used to treat muscle spasms as well as other conditions, such as anxiety disorders. At my next appointment, I admitted that after my back had healed, I sometimes used the Valium just to feel better. I also said I'd started to believe I was bipolar. I asked the doctor to refer me to a psychiatrist. There were only two on the island, but he was able to get me an appointment with one of them.

Diagnosis

Shortly after, I received a call from the Dr. Nakamura. During our discussion, he asked whether I used drugs or alcohol. I told him I drank two to three glasses of wine per night. Would I be willing to stop drinking during treatment? I said sure.

At our first appointment, I explained why I wanted his help. I said something like, "I don't need a diagnosis, but I'm not afraid of one. I don't need medication, but I'm willing to try it. What I need is for my results to change. For almost five years, I've been busting my butt, working hard and being the best person I can be, but I'm no farther ahead than when I began. It's crushing my spirit."

I shared that I thought I was bipolar. The doctor asked me to give examples of incidents that I viewed as manic episodes. The two that I shared were both related to courses I had taken in a self-development program (which I now consider a cult). He said, "Have you had anything you'd call manic that wasn't associated with the influence of this group?" I searched my mind and said, "No."

The doctor pulled out a couple of screening tests and had me answer the questions. As he reviewed my answers, he asked me what I knew about ADHD. I told him I didn't know much. I associated that disorder with people who couldn't focus, and I had never been accused of an inability to focus. He explained that hyperfocus is one way ADHD can show itself, but it can also result in an inability to succeed at things fully. That sounded relevant to me.

The doctor encouraged me to order and read the book *Driven to Distraction* by Edward M. Hallowell and John J. Ratey. The book includes a list of "Suggested Diagnostic Criteria for Attention Deficit Disorder in Adults." The authors based the criteria on symptoms commonly reported to them by their patients. Here's a summary of the main points:

A. A chronic disturbance in which at least fifteen of the following are present:

1. A sense of underachievement, of not meeting one's goals (regardless of how much one has actually accomplished). . . .

2. Difficulty getting organized. . . .

3. Chronic procrastination or trouble getting started. . . .

4. Many projects going simultaneously; trouble with follow-through. . . .

5. Tendency to say what comes to mind without considering the timing or appropriateness of the remark. . . .

6. A frequent search for high stimulation. . . .

7. An intolerance of boredom. . . .

8. Easy distractibility, trouble focusing attention, tendency to tune out or drift away in the middle of a page or a conversation, often coupled with an ability to hyperfocus at times. . . .

9. Often creative, intuitive, highly intelligent. . . .

10. Trouble in going through established channels, following "proper" procedure. . . .

11. Impatient; low tolerance for frustration. . . .

12. Impulsive, either verbally or in action, as in impulsive spending of money, changing plans, enacting new schemes or career plans, and the like. . . .

13. Tendency to worry needlessly, endlessly; tendency to scan the horizon looking for something to worry about, alternating with inattention to or disregard for actual dangers. . . .

14. Sense of insecurity. . . .

15. Mood swings . . . especially when disengaged from a person or a project. . . .

16. Restlessness. . . .

17. Tendency toward addictive behaviors such as gambling, shopping, eating, or overwork; or toward addictive substances such as alcohol, cocaine. . . .

18. Chronic problems with self-esteem. . . .

19. Inaccurate self-observation. . . .

B. Childhood history of ADD. (It may not have been formally diagnosed, but in reviewing the history, the signs and symptoms must have been there.)

C. Situation not explained by other medical or psychiatric condition.

Criteria B and C really didn't resonate with me. But in list A, I identified with sixteen of the symptoms. Looking back, if I'd had the courage to ask Philip to evaluate me, he probably could have given evidence for all the items on that list.

At last I knew about my mental illness. I was diagnosed with depression, anxiety, and ADHD. Something was beginning to unravel in a good way.

Learning About Myself

The psychiatrist and I started talk therapy on week two. When we examined aspects of my childhood and growing up, I could spot signs of depressed mood going back to around age three. Some environmental factors in my family had contributed—divorced parents, their struggle, financial insecurity—but not all the signs were environmental. Some of them pointed to something built in, something I identified as "me." And although I don't in any way mean to throw my family under the bus, an honest assessment clearly showed indicators of untreated mental illness on both sides of my family. Neither family had reference points for admitting this or managing mental illness in conventional ways.

As I looked back at my life, I saw other signs potentially related to mental illness. Throughout school, there were times when I definitely got upset in very dramatic, emotional ways. I wasn't good at "rolling with the punches." Being gay and mostly closeted for about twenty years of life was also a factor. Not being able to feel open and honest added to my physical causes of depression and anxiety.

My college years were a really compelling period that had never made sense to me until viewed through the lens of depression. After attending for two years and doing pretty well, I had a kind of quiet breakdown. I had financial struggles and had missed the deadline for financial aid applications. It never dawned on me that I could go to the financial aid office and ask for an exception. I told no one. I later understood that this is an example of social distancing, which many people with mental illness experience.

There were other friction points during college. Working as a singing waiter on a dinner cruise ship gave me an artistic life in which I felt open and accepted. But because the university I attended was extremely conservative, I felt like I had to hide who I was. I also was questioning my major, and didn't see anything in the school's curriculum that seemed like a better choice for me. Rather than getting help or talking to a therapist, I made a big decision and announced it to everyone: School was not for me. I dropped out to pursue a more artistic career. Some parts of this experience were true to the real me, but it was all clouded by a fog of depression. If I'd been able to reach out, talk to people, and get help, I might have found less dramatic solutions.

Starting Medication

Many of the thoughts I had about psychiatric medication related to negative things people said, outdated media images of older psychiatric treatments, and pop culture references like the movies *One Flew Over the Cuckoo's Nest* and *Girl, Interrupted*. My ideas were based more on rumors and extreme cases in the media rather than anything true.

Nevertheless, I had many fears about medication. I was worried about possible side effects and whether I would feel numbed or "checked out."

I even consulted a medium about my concerns. I had done phone sessions with this person about once a year, and the guidance I received from her always seemed timely and relevant. She often gave me advice about personal care, dietary habits, and nature-related recommendations, like taking walks with specific instructions. This time, when I queried about mental illness and psychiatric issues, she responded that yes, there was something up with my brain chemistry. She said I'd probably benefit from taking an antidepressant, and that being sensitive, I'd probably need a relatively low dose. I asked if this was temporary or permanent. She responded, "It's undetermined."

At my next session with my psychiatrist, I asked, "Are we ever going to talk about medication and whether I should try it?" We discussed it the following week, and he put me on a relatively new antidepressant, desvenlafaxine.

I read all the potential side effects and planned to take my first dose the next morning. At dinner, I said to Philip, "I want to give this a month and see how it goes. Please don't comment unless you think something dangerous is happening. But please also pay attention. Let's touch base when the month is up." He agreed.

The next morning, and for the whole first month, I put my pill in my hand and said a silent prayer: "God, I need this to work. Please consecrate this medicine to my health. I really can't stand any major side effects. So be it." Then I'd take my pill.

On day one, after a mostly sleepless night, I convinced myself I was having a manic episode—a side effect that the medication triggers in some people. I was panicking about the potential effects and the way I felt. Eventually I took out a piece of paper and wrote down all my thoughts, something like this: "Antidepressants are bad. They're for lazy people. They'll kill you. What if I've been given the wrong medication and am bipolar? It's a conspiracy by the pharmaceutical companies." And on and on and on. I filled up almost a whole page.

After getting all this out, I seemed to calm down and was able to rest. I'd never been on any medication long-term, so this triggered all my subconscious beliefs about medications *and* about medications related to psychiatric health.

Early the next morning, I explained the situation to my psychiatrist on the phone. He left it up to me: If I wanted to discontinue the medication, I could. If I wanted to give it a couple of days, I could do that too. Having the option to not take the medication put my mind at ease. I persevered.

Effects of Medication

Within just a couple of days, I felt remarkably different. The cloud of darkness and cynicism that had seemed to pervade my thinking and attitude lifted. Previously, I had thought I was just being realistic. Without that cloud, I realized I had been experiencing depression. At my next psychiatric session, my doctor explained how a compromised limbic system—a part of the brain—can color the way one views the whole world.

Within a couple of weeks, I had a whole new sense of my demeanor. I was feeling hopeful, making progress at work, and becoming more engaged in improving my own life. In addition to the medication, strategies I read for how to manage depression and ADHD also helped me.

A month passed, and it was time to discuss the situation with Philip. I remember sitting at the kitchen table after dinner that night. I said, "Here's my experience: Let's say how I feel and my attitude in the day are an elevator in a building. Before, it wasn't uncommon for me to make several trips to the basement during the day, and it took a lot of mental effort to get the elevator out of the basement and above ground. The only difference I feel with the medicine is that I start above ground and don't really go to the basement at all." Philip agreed with this analogy, and he mentioned that a heaviness that had usually seemed to be pervasive with me was gone. Together, we agreed it was a good idea to continue the medication.

Managing my mental illness wasn't a perfect journey. A few months in, I started to feel depressed again and mentioned it to my psychiatrist. He was happy I'd caught it. He doubled my dose of the antidepressant, which seemed to do the trick. After a period, I went back down to the original dosage.

The medication was not without side effects, though none were major. Sleep was a little more difficult, and I sweat and get heated more easily than I did before medication. I also gained some weight—probably ten to fifteen pounds, which is common with antidepressants. With that said, I also entered middle age, so some of these side effects might also be natural signs of aging.

When I was on the higher doses of antidepressant, I started to experience some sexual dysfunction for the first time in my life. I spoke to my doctor and got an as-needed prescription for Cialis (tadalafil). That handled the bulk of the problem, and things continued to improve when I was able to reduce my dosage of antidepressant.

A friend of mine who was also struggling with depression asked her psychiatrist to try the same antidepressant I was taking. She had very negative side effects and was taken off it within a couple of weeks. I include this to point out the importance of working with a trained professional to find the right treatment plan for you. There is no "one size fits all" approach to mental illness.

I've been stable on my medication for almost a decade. My psychiatrist and I have talked about reducing the dosage and then going off the antidepressant altogether to see if I still need it. For now, I err on the side of caution. I'll probably try this experiment at some point. But if it's not successful, I'm comfortable being on this medication for the rest of my life in order to keep my mental stability. The side effects I experience are insignificant compared to the good effects that have blossomed in my life from treating my mental illness.

My Life Since Treatment

I'm currently a success story of routine mental health treatment. On a day-to-day basis, I don't feel depressed at all. Like everyone, I occasionally have a bad day, but they are few and far between.

As I mentioned at the beginning of this book, I've become more successful since I began managing my mental illness. I lost my time-share sales job, but after several false starts, I found a new career in insurance that I love and that pays well. I finally finished my college degree—not because I need it for my current career, but to make right a promise to myself that I had broken. Our finances are in good shape. I work out more than I ever have in my life. If I hadn't sought treatment for mental illness, I doubt I would have had the energy or focus to accomplish these goals.

Philip and I even survived six months to a year of a time when we thought we might split up. We successfully navigated couples counseling and my temporary sexual dysfunction. We worked out some of the kinks between us and gained greater communication skills. We committed more deeply to each other, and I love him more than I ever have. He tells me the same, and I trust him. I doubt I'd have made it through that process if I were still exhibiting signs of clinical depression.

I resumed drinking alcohol at some point, but I pay attention and deliberately cut back when a third or fourth drink becomes too common. Philip has permission to tell me "no more" or "you've been drinking a little too much lately," and I rein it in. I mention this so you'll know I'm not perfect. I'm human. But I do pay attention to whether my habits add to any sense of depression or negatively affect my life. Rarely is the answer yes, but when it is, I adjust appropriately. I pay attention to my mental health so I can manage it.

Speaking Up and Coming Out

Living in a culture that stigmatizes mental illness, my first reaction was to avoid admitting or discussing my depression, anxiety, and ADHD. But as my life improved, I became more comfortable with speaking up and coming out as mentally ill.

I realized more and more how uneducated I had previously been and how I had maligned people seeking help for mental illness, especially through medication. As I came to terms with this, I started to speak up to repair some of the damage I had done. I encouraged therapy when people were having hard times. If anything negative was said about being treated for mental illness, I was quick to point out that I was on antidepressants and I'd had good results. I pushed back when people tried to shame me by foolishly saying that if I'd just eat organic foods or exercise more, I could handle it "naturally." I explained how many years I had tortured myself with these types of thoughts and that I'd had very poor results from not embracing conventional treatment. Over time, I fully came out as mentally ill.

Conclusion

Life can be hard for everyone, in varying ways and to varying degrees. I don't have any agenda for what you or anyone else should do, other than take care of yourself better, if you can. Use any tools that might help make it easier to enjoy getting through the day, to rack up successes, and to get along with the people around you and society as a whole. I believe only when we individually feel sane do we have a chance of improving some of our shared insanity.

Stories are significant to finding meaning in our lives. Thank you for allowing me to share my story with you.

12

EVERYONE IS CRAZY

THE TITLE OF this chapter is not factually accurate, and it uses stigmatizing language. Yet it helps me to keep this quiet belief conscious in my mind.

Telling myself that everyone is crazy is a kindness I extend to myself and others. It's not an accusation. It's a way of letting people off the hook, of releasing the pressure, of not judging so harshly. It's giving everyone a break. In a strange way, it also makes me feel more connected to humanity.

My husband Philip isn't under psychiatric care, but he has often enjoyed the benefits of talk therapy one to two times per month. When he found the right psychologist that he connected with, she presented him with this short piece excerpted from Elizabeth Lesser's 2004 book *Broken Open: How Difficult Times Can Help Us Grow*. I've been granted permission to reproduce it here.

Bozos on the Bus

*We're all bozos on this bus, so we might as well
sit back and enjoy the ride.*

—Wavy Gravy

One of my heroes is the clown-activist Wavy Gravy. He is best known for a role that he played in 1969, when he was the master of ceremonies at the Woodstock festival. Since then, he's been a social activist, a major "fun-d"- raiser for good causes, a Ben & Jerry's ice-cream flavor, an unofficial hospital chaplain, and the founder of a camp for inner-city kids. . . . "Like the best of clowns," wrote a reporter in *The Village Voice*, "Wavy Gravy makes as big a fool of himself as is necessary to make a wiser man of you." . . .

But my all-time favorite Wavy-ism is the line . . . about bozos on the bus. . . . I believe that we *are* all bozos on the bus, contrary to the self-assured image we work so hard to present to each other on a daily basis. We are all half-baked experiments—mistake-prone beings, born without an instruction book into a complex world. None of us are models of perfect behavior: We have all betrayed and been betrayed; we've been known to be egotistical, unreliable, lethargic, and stingy; and each one of us has, at times, awakened in the middle of the night worrying about everything from money, kids, or terrorism to wrinkled skin and receding hairlines. In other words, we're all bozos on the bus.

This, in my opinion, is cause for celebration. If we're all bozos, then . . . we can put down the burden of pretense and get on with being bozos. We can approach the problems that visit bozo-type beings without the usual embarrassment and resistance. It is so much more effective to work on our rough edges with a light and forgiving heart. Imagine how freeing it would be to take a more compassionate and comedic view of the human condition—not as a way to deny our defects but as a way to welcome them as part of the standard human operating system. Every single person on this bus called Earth hurts; it's when we have shame about our failings that hurt turns into suffering. In our shame, we feel outcast, as if there is another bus somewhere, rolling along on a smooth road. Its passengers are all thin, healthy, happy, well-dressed, and well-liked people who belong to harmonious families, hold jobs that don't bore or aggravate them, and never do mean things, or goofy things like forget where they parked their car, lose their wallet, or say something totally inappropriate. We long to be on that bus with the other normal people.

But we are on the bus that says bozo on the front, and we worry that we may be the only passenger onboard. This is the illusion that so many of us labor under—that we're all alone in our weirdness and our uncertainty; that we may be the most lost person on the highway. Of course we don't always feel like this. Sometimes a wave of self-forgiveness washes over us, and suddenly we're connected to our fellow humans; suddenly we belong.

It is wonderful to take your place on the bus with the other bozos. It may be the first step to enlightenment to understand with all of your brain cells that the other bus—that sleek bus with the cool people who know where they are going—is also filled with bozos: bozos in drag, bozos with secrets. When we see clearly that every single human being, regardless of fame or fortune or age or brains or beauty, shares the same ordinary foibles, a strange thing happens. We begin to cheer up, to loosen up, and we become as buoyant as those people we imagined on the other bus. As we rumble along the potholed road, lost as ever, through the valleys and over the hills, we find ourselves among friends. We sit back, and enjoy the ride.

I hope you're more able to enjoy the bus ride after reading this book. I hope my story has touched you and that the information I've provided will help you. If you or someone else can take a little better care of yourself and not feel shameful about coming out as mentally ill, I will feel that my life has had more purpose. (Shameless self-promotion: If this book does help you in any way, give it a good review online!)

If you'd like to share any of your mental health successes or your own story of coming out as mentally ill, contact me at *www.comingoutasmentallyill.com*. If I get enough interesting stories, I'm committed to share them in a follow-up book.

ENDNOTES

1. "What Is Mental Illness?" American Psychiatric Association, 2018, www.psychiatry.org/patients-families/what-is-mental-illness.

2. "Mental Health: A State of Well-being," World Health Organization, August 2014, www.who.int/features/factfiles/mental_health/en.

3. "Know the Warning Signs," National Alliance on Mental Illness, www.nami.org/learn-more/know-the-warning-signs.

4. Ibid.

5. "Mental Health by the Numbers," National Alliance on Mental Illness, 2019, www.nami.org/learn-more/mental-health-by-the-numbers.

6. "10 Leading Causes of Death, United States," Centers for Disease Control, https://webappa.cdc.gov/cgi-bin/broker.exe.

7. "Why Is the Trump Presidency of Extreme Psychological Interest?" Psychology Today,

https://www.psychologytoday.com/us/basics/
president-donald-trump.

8. "Mental Health by the Numbers," National Alliance
on Mental Illness, 2019, www.nami.org/
learn-more/mental-health-by-the-numbers.

9. "World Health Report: Mental Disorders Affect One
in Four People," World Health Organization, Oct.
4, 2001, www.who.int/whr/2001/media_centre/
press_release/en.

10. Ibid. (The full report, The World Health Report
2001—Mental Health: New Understanding, New
Hope, can be found at www.who.int/whr/2001/
en.)

11. "Mental Health Conditions," National Alliance
on Mental Illness, www.nami.org/learn-more/
mental-health-conditions.

12. "What Are Personality Disorders?" American
Psychiatric Association, www.psychiatry.
org/patients-families/personality-disorders/
what-are-personality-disorders.

13. "Substance Use and Mental Health," National
Institute of Mental Health, www.nimh.nih.gov/
health/topics/substance-use-and-mental-health/
index.shtml.

14. Ibid.

15. "Causes of Mental Illness," WebMD,
www.webmd.com/mental-health/
mental-health-causes-mental-illness.

16. Ibid.

17. Richard J. McNally, What Is Mental Illness? (Cambridge, MA: Belknap Press, 2012).

18. Amir M. Kalali, "Audacious Advances to Discover New Treatments for Psychiatric Brain Disorders," Current Psychiatry 17, no. 3 (March 2018): 8, 10–11.

19. "Complementary Health Approaches," National Alliance on Mental Illness, www.nami.org/Learn-More/Treatment/Complementary-Health-Approaches.

20. "ECT, TMS and Other Brain Stimulation Theraparies," National Alliance on Mental Illness, www.nami.org/Learn-More/Treatment/ECT,-TMS-and-Other-Brain-Stimulation-Therapies.

21. Stephen Ross et al., "Rapid and Sustained Symptom Reduction Following Psilocybin Treatment for Anxiety and Depression in Patients with Life-Threatening Cancer: A Randomized Controlled Trial," Journal of Psychopharmacology 30, no. 12 (Dec. 2016): 1165–1180, https://journals.sagepub.com/doi/full/10.1177/0269881116675512.

22. Wulf Rössler, "The Stigma of Mental Disorders," EMBO Reports 17 (2016): 1250–53.

23. Michael Friedman, "The Stigma of Mental Illness Is Making Us Sicker," Psychology Today, May 13, 2014, www.

psychologytoday.com/us/blog/brick-brick/201405/
the-stigma-mental-illness-is-making-us-sicker.

24. Luna Greenstein, "9 Ways to Fight Mental Health
    Stigma," National Alliance on Mental Illness, Oct.
    11, 2017, www.nami.org/blogs/nami-blog/october-
    2017/9-ways-to-fight-mental-health-stigma.

25. Chris Naylor et al., Bringing Together Physical and
    Mental Health: A New Frontier for Integrated Care
    (King's Fund, March 2016), www.kingsfund.org.
    uk/publications/physical-and-mental-health.

26. "10 Priorities for Integrating Physical and Mental
    Health," King's Fund, www.kingsfund.org.
    uk/publications/physical-and-mental-health/
    priorities-for-integrating.

27. "About Mental Health America," www.mhanational.
    org/about.

28. "Staying Well When You Have a Mental Illness,"
    Mental Health America, https://www.mhanational.
    org/sites/default/files/staying_well1.pdf.

29. Lara Honos-Webb, "The Gift of ADHD
    Controversy," Psychology Today, March 18,
    2013, www.psychologytoday.com/us/blog/
    the-gift-adhd/201303/the-gift-adhd-controversy.

30. Tracy Shawn, "The Upside of Downside:
    The Surprising Gifts of Mental Disorders,"
    PsychCentral, July 8, 2018, https://psychcentral.
    com/blog/the-upside-of-downside-the-surprising-
    gifts-of-mental-disorders.

31. Jonah Lehrer, "The Upside of Autism," Wall Street Journal, March 31, 2012, www.wsj.com/articles/ SB100014240527023038165045773074919336 71470, quoted in Shawn, "Upside of Downside."

RECOMMENDED RESOURCES

Hallowell, Edward M., and John J. Ratey. *Driven to Distraction: Recognizing and Coping with Attention Deficit Disorder from Childhood through Adulthood.* Revised ed. New York: Anchor Books, 2011.

Lesser, Elizabeth. Broken Open: How Difficult Times Can Help Us Grow. New York: Villard Books, 2004.

McNally, Richard J. *What Is Mental Illness?* Cambridge, MA: Belknap Press, 2012.

Mental Health America, www.mhanational.org.

National Alliance on Mental Illness, www.nami.org.

National Institute of Mental Health, www.nimh.nih.gov.